I0018409

A WORD OF THANKS

Thank you for purchasing this book and supporting the work of independent creators. Your encouragement fuels the creativity and passion behind every project we undertake at NineTwo Creations.

As a token of our appreciation, we'd like to invite you to explore our merchandise at www.ninetwocreations.com. Whether you're looking for something unique for yourself or a gift for someone special, we're excited to offer **free shipping** on your order. Simply use the promo code **BOOK** at checkout.

Your support means the world to us, and we're thrilled to have you as part of our growing community. Thank you for being a part of this journey. Here's to the stories we tell, the ideas we share, and the futures we build together!

— NineTwo Creations

GETTING STARTED IN STREAMING

MASTER THE ART OF LIVE STREAMING AND CONNECT WITH YOUR FUTURE FOLLOWERS

BY

Jordan Vance

© Copyright 2024 by NineTwo Creations L.L.C. - All rights reserved.

It is not legal to reproduce, duplicate, or transmit any part of this document in either electronic means or printed format. Recording of this publication is strictly prohibited.

First Edition

Published by NineTwo Creations L.L.C.

For permission requests, contact the publisher at ninetwocreations@gmail.com

This book is intended for informational purposes only. The author and publisher make no representations or warranties regarding the accuracy, applicability, or completeness of the contents. The reader is advised to consult with a professional where appropriate.

TABLE OF CONTENTS

Introduction

Hi, I'm Jordan Vance. Over the years, I've immersed myself in the world of live streaming, observing, learning, and researching what works and, just as importantly, what doesn't when it comes to building a successful streaming presence. My journey began with a deep curiosity about how some streamers rise to stardom while others struggle to find their footing. Since then, I've turned that curiosity into a mission: helping aspiring and growing streamers carve their own paths in this dynamic and competitive industry.

I've worked with countless creators—newcomers who are hitting the "Go Live" button for the first time and seasoned streamers looking to refine their strategy. As a mentor and advisor, I've seen firsthand the common hurdles streamers face, from technical challenges to audience engagement struggles, and I've developed practical, actionable solutions to overcome them. My goal is to guide you through this process with the clarity and confidence needed to succeed.

In *Getting Started in Streaming: Master the Art of Live Streaming and Connect with Your Future Followers*, I've distilled my knowledge and experience into a comprehensive guide. Whether you're dreaming of building a community, showcasing your passions, or turning streaming into a career, this book is your roadmap. We'll explore everything from setting up your first stream to engaging with your audience and sustaining long-term success.

The world of streaming is vibrant, exciting, and full of opportunity. But it's also a space that demands preparation, perseverance, and a willingness to learn. By the end of this book, you'll not only understand the tools and strategies to thrive in streaming but also feel equipped to tackle challenges and make meaningful connections with your audience.

Let's get started on this journey together. Your audience is out there waiting—now it's your time to shine.

Chapter 1: Understanding the World of Streaming

If you've ever wondered what draws millions of people to watch someone play video games, paint a canvas, or even cook dinner in real time, you're not alone. Live streaming has become a global phenomenon, reshaping how we share experiences and connect with others. It's no longer just about broadcasting—it's about building communities, creating moments, and sharing passions in ways that feel personal and immediate.

Consider this: 27% of all internet users tune in to live streams weekly. That's over a quarter of the world's online population engaging with creators who are sharing their lives, skills, and creativity in real time. This incredible statistic highlights a fundamental truth—people crave connection and authenticity, and live streaming delivers both in spades.

What's more, the platforms hosting these streams have exploded in variety and accessibility. Twitch, the original powerhouse for gamers, has expanded to all sorts of content, from art tutorials to talk shows. YouTube Live offers creators the chance to engage with their existing subscribers in an interactive format. TikTok LIVE has brought the spontaneity of live streaming to mobile-first audiences, while even business-focused LinkedIn has entered the scene, enabling professionals to live stream conferences, webinars, and more.

The beauty of live streaming lies in its simplicity: anyone with a phone or computer can go live and connect with the world. It's raw, it's unfiltered, and it's incredibly powerful. This chapter will explore how streaming has become a force in the digital age, why it resonates with so many, and what makes it a compelling opportunity for you.

Streaming appeals to people for all sorts of reasons, and the motivations behind hitting that "Go Live" button are as varied as the content being streamed. For many, it's about building an audience—finding like-minded individuals who share a passion for gaming, art, fitness, or just good conversation. Others see it as a chance to share their passions, whether that's teaching guitar chords, painting landscapes, or cooking intricate recipes. And then there are those who dream of turning streaming into a full-time job, creating a career out of doing what they love.

But here's the thing: live streaming isn't an instant ticket to fame or fortune. One of the most common misconceptions is that all you need to succeed is a camera and charisma. In reality, the path to success in streaming takes time, consistency, and a bit of trial and error. You don't have to start with a Hollywood-level studio or top-tier gaming rig. Some of the most successful streamers began with little more than a basic webcam, a budget microphone, and a lot of passion.

That said, unrealistic expectations can derail your efforts before they even start. Overnight success stories are rare, and the reality is that building an audience often requires months—or even years—of dedication. The key is to set realistic goals from the outset. Maybe your initial aim is to connect with five viewers who enjoy your content or to stream consistently twice a week. These small, manageable targets help build momentum and lay the foundation for long-term success.

Streaming is a journey, not a sprint. Whether you're in it for the fun of sharing your hobbies or with dreams of going pro, the first step is setting a solid, realistic foundation. This is what separates those who burn out quickly from those who build something lasting.

Live streaming is more than just a digital trend; it's a powerful way to share your voice, your passions, and your creativity with the world. Whether you see it as a fun hobby, a creative outlet, or even the first step toward a full-fledged career, the possibilities are as limitless as your imagination. The beauty of streaming lies in its versatility—you can shape it into whatever you want it to be.

The best part? You don't need to have it all figured out before you start. Some of the most successful streamers began with modest setups and uncertain goals, learning and growing along the way. What matters most is the willingness to take that first step, embrace the journey, and remain open to experimenting with what works for you.

In the chapters ahead, we'll dive into the tools, strategies, and mindset you need to get started. From setting up your first stream to finding and engaging your audience, you'll discover how to turn your streaming ambitions into a reality. The world is waiting for your story—are you ready to share it?

Chapter 2: Setting Goals and Defining Your Niche

Before you even press that "Go Live" button for the first time, there's one critical thing to figure out: Why are you streaming? This might sound simple, but having a clear purpose is what separates a casual experiment from a lasting, rewarding endeavor. Streaming without a goal is like heading out on a road trip without a map—sure, it might be fun at first, but you're likely to end up lost or frustrated along the way.

Your goals can be as big or as small as you want them to be, but they should give you direction. Some people stream to build a community, to find others who share their passions, whether that's gaming, cooking, or even knitting. Others want to showcase a specific skill—turning their expertise in graphic design, fitness training, or language learning into something engaging and interactive. And then there are those who approach streaming as a way to make money—through sponsorships, subscriptions, or viewer support—dreaming of turning their passion into a full-time career.

Let's look at an example: Imagine you love playing retro video games. If your goal is to build a community, your stream might focus on encouraging conversation with your audience, swapping favorite gaming memories, and keeping the vibe nostalgic and welcoming. On the other hand, if your goal is to monetize your stream, you might need to plan differently— building a more polished brand, connecting with retro game publishers for sponsorships, or tailoring your schedule for maximum viewer engagement.

The beauty of live streaming is that it's flexible—you can mold it to match your goals. But clarity is key. Without a defined purpose, it's easy to fall into the trap of comparing yourself to others or trying to copy what's already out there. That's a recipe for frustration. Instead, think of your goal as the north star guiding your streaming journey. It will help you make decisions, stay motivated, and keep your content focused.

When it comes to streaming, everyone's "why" looks a little different. For some, it's the thrill of building an audience—creating a space where people with shared interests can come together. This might mean cultivating a loyal group of gamers who cheer you on during your toughest matches or assembling a virtual classroom of viewers eager to learn from your tutorials. The joy of knowing your stream makes someone's day a little better can be incredibly rewarding.

Others stream because they're passionate about sharing their talents and hobbies. Maybe you're an artist who wants to show the process behind your creations, or a musician looking to perform live and connect with fans in real-time. Streaming lets you take what you love and bring it to life for an audience, turning solo activities into collaborative experiences.

For a growing number of people, streaming is about building a career. And while that might mean financial success, it's also about creating something sustainable and meaningful. Platforms like Twitch, YouTube, and TikTok offer revenue opportunities through ads, subscriptions, sponsorships, and donations, making it possible to turn streaming into a full-time job—or at least a side hustle. But make no mistake: success in streaming is a marathon, not a sprint.

One of the biggest misconceptions about streaming is that it's an instant path to fame. You might see stories of overnight sensations who racked up thousands of followers seemingly out of nowhere, but for most streamers, the road to success is paved with patience and consistency. Viewers don't just stumble onto your stream—they stick around because they see your dedication, authenticity, and effort over time.

Another myth? That you need expensive gear to get started. Sure, some streamers have setups that look straight out of a professional studio, but many started with little more than a basic webcam and microphone. The quality of your content and your connection with your audience matters far more than how fancy your setup looks.

The key to thriving in the streaming world is to set realistic expectations and achievable goals. Instead of focusing on how many viewers you'll have by the end of your first week, think about the habits you'll build. Can you commit to a regular streaming schedule? Can you engage with every viewer who drops in, even if it's just one or two at first? Small wins, like improving your presentation skills or building relationships with early viewers, lay the groundwork for bigger milestones.

Streaming isn't a get-rich-quick scheme or a shortcut to fame. It's a journey of growth, experimentation, and connection. And when you approach it with the right mindset, it can be one of the most fulfilling creative outlets you'll ever explore.

The first step to building a successful streaming journey is to clearly define your goals. What do you want to achieve with your stream? Perhaps it's building a community of like-minded people who share your interests, such as gaming, art, or fitness. Or maybe you're looking to share a unique skill or talent—something that will educate, entertain, or inspire your viewers. For others, the goal might be to create a career, earning an income from streaming through sponsorships, subscriptions, or donations. Whatever your motivation, having a clear purpose will guide every decision you make, from the content you create to how you interact with your audience.

Once you've identified your goal, it's equally important to define your niche—the unique angle or focus that sets you apart. Think about what excites you and how you can turn that passion into a compelling experience for your viewers. For example, if you're passionate about gaming, what type of games will you stream? Are you drawn to competitive esports, nostalgic retro titles, or engaging storytelling in RPGs? Similarly, if you're into fitness, will you focus on quick home workouts, yoga tutorials, or live Q&A sessions on health and nutrition? Your niche is where your personal enthusiasm intersects with what your audience finds valuable.

It's also crucial to approach streaming with realistic expectations. Many aspiring streamers fall into the trap of expecting instant success, believing they'll attract thousands of viewers right away. The truth is, building an audience takes time, effort, and patience. Instead of fixating on metrics like follower counts or earnings, focus on what you can control. Set achievable goals, like streaming consistently on specific days or engaging meaningfully with every viewer who drops by your channel. These small, deliberate actions create the foundation for long-term growth and help you build habits that lead to success.

With a clear goal, a defined niche, and realistic expectations, you're ready to start transforming your ideas into action. But before you go live, you'll need to prepare. In the next chapter, we'll dive into the art of planning your stream—crafting outlines, managing your time, and ensuring every session runs smoothly. Because every successful stream begins with a solid plan.

Chapter 3: Planning Your Stream

When you think of live streaming, it's easy to imagine something spontaneous—a natural flow of interaction between a streamer and their audience. And while spontaneity is a big part of what makes live streaming exciting, the truth is that the best streams often have one thing in common: preparation. Planning is the backbone of a successful stream, even if it's not obvious to viewers. Without a plan, streams can feel aimless, chaotic, or unprofessional, and that can quickly drive away potential followers.

The level of planning you'll need depends on your goals and style. A casual stream might just require a mental outline of topics to cover or activities to share, allowing for a relaxed, impromptu vibe. But if you're aiming for professional quality, your planning will need to go deeper—outlines, scripts, segment transitions, and even backup plans for when things don't go as expected. Professional streamers know that preparation allows them to focus on delivering great content without being distracted by avoidable hiccups.

Think of planning as creating a safety net for your creativity. By organizing your ideas ahead of time, you free yourself to focus on engaging with your audience in the moment. Whether you're streaming gameplay, hosting a live tutorial, or running a Q&A, having a plan keeps you on track and ensures your stream offers value to viewers from start to finish.

Creating a plan for your stream doesn't mean scripting every moment—it's about finding the right balance between structure and spontaneity. The level of detail will depend on the type of stream you're running, but the core idea is to prepare enough so that your stream feels engaging and professional, while still leaving room for organic interactions with your audience.

Start by crafting an outline or script tailored to your stream type. For instance, if you're hosting a gaming stream, your outline might include checkpoints like introducing the game, sharing your goals for the session, and taking breaks to engage with the chat. On the other hand, if you're running a tutorial or educational stream, you might want a more detailed script to ensure you explain concepts clearly and in a logical order. Outlines can be as simple as bullet points or as detailed as a full written script—whatever helps you feel confident and in control.

When planning your stream, consider how to keep it engaging from start to finish. Start strong with a welcoming introduction that grabs attention—acknowledge your audience, set the tone, and give a quick rundown of what they can expect. Break your content into manageable segments to maintain variety and keep viewers interested. For example, a gaming stream might alternate between gameplay and answering chat questions, while an art stream could combine live drawing with discussions about techniques or tools. By mixing up the pace and content, you reduce the risk of losing your audience's attention.

Time management is another critical element of planning. Live streams often run longer than expected, and it's easy to get carried away in the moment. Set a loose timeline for your stream, including how long you'll spend on each segment. This helps ensure your content feels cohesive and prevents you from running out of material too early. Tools like countdown timers or pre-set reminders can help you stay on track without interrupting the flow of your stream.

Of course, even the best plans can hit unexpected roadblocks. Technical issues like dropped internet connections, audio glitches, or software crashes are common challenges for streamers. Prepare contingency plans, such as having a backup game, an alternate activity, or even a simple "standby" screen to display while you troubleshoot. Equally important is being ready for lulls in audience engagement—prepare a few questions, stories, or topics to fill the gaps if chat activity slows down. The more prepared you are, the more confident you'll feel in handling the unexpected.

Ultimately, a well-planned stream is not just about controlling every moment—it's about creating a framework that allows you to focus on what matters most: connecting with your audience and delivering a great experience.

Planning may not seem as exciting as the actual act of streaming, but it's the foundation that transforms a good idea into a memorable experience. When you take the time to outline your content, manage your time effectively, and prepare for potential challenges, you're setting yourself up for success. A thoughtful plan not only helps you feel more confident when you go live but also ensures that your audience stays engaged and enjoys the value you're delivering.

The key takeaway is this: preparation doesn't stifle creativity—it enhances it. A well-planned stream allows you to focus on being present with your audience instead of scrambling to figure out what's next. And the more you plan, the more seamless and natural your streams will feel over time.

With your planning skills honed, it's time to take the next step in building your streaming setup. In the next chapter, we'll dive into the equipment and tools you'll need to bring your vision to life. From microphones to webcams to optimizing your internet connection, you'll learn how to create a setup that works for your goals and budget. Let's get your stream ready to shine!

Chapter 4: Building Your Streaming Setup

Your streaming setup is the backbone of your content. It's what ensures your voice is heard, your visuals are crisp, and your stream runs smoothly. Whether you're starting with a simple arrangement or aiming for a professional-grade setup, the good news is that you can begin streaming without breaking the bank—and upgrade as you grow.

At its core, a functional streaming setup includes four essential components: a reliable PC or laptop, a quality microphone, a decent webcam, and a strong internet connection. These are the building blocks that make your stream watchable and engaging. But not every setup has to look the same.

For beginners, a minimal setup might mean using an everyday laptop, a basic USB microphone, and a built-in webcam or an affordable external camera. This kind of setup is more than enough to test the waters and see what streaming feels like. On the other hand, professional streamers often invest in dedicated streaming PCs or rigs, high-end microphones like the Blue Yeti, DSLR cameras adapted for live use, and even studio lighting to create polished, high-quality content.

The beauty of streaming is that it's scalable. You can start with what you have and gradually upgrade as your audience grows and your goals evolve. The key is knowing where to prioritize your investment early on to get the best results for your budget and content style.

When it comes to building your streaming setup, the devil is in the details. Each piece of hardware plays a role in the overall quality of your stream, and understanding what works for your needs can make all the difference.

Your PC or laptop is the engine of your streaming setup, and its capabilities determine the quality and smoothness of your stream. For lighter content, like casual chatting or art streams, most modern laptops will do just fine. However, gaming or high-resolution streams require more power. At a minimum, aim for a system with an Intel i5 or AMD Ryzen 5 processor, 8GB of RAM (though 16GB is highly recommended), and a dedicated GPU such as the Nvidia GTX 1660 or better. These specs will ensure you can manage your streaming software and basic gaming without significant performance issues.

That said, if you plan to stream demanding games while running a single-PC setup, you'll need higher-end hardware. Games with intensive graphics and fast action, such as AAA titles or competitive esports games, require a stronger GPU, more RAM, and a higher-performing CPU to handle both gameplay and encoding simultaneously. If your budget allows, consider building or investing in a custom PC tailored for gaming and streaming, with room to grow as your content demands increase.

For those who want the ultimate setup, a dual-PC configuration can offer significant advantages. By splitting the workload—one PC for gaming and the other for streaming—you can ensure a lag-free experience for both you and your audience. While this option requires a larger budget and additional equipment like a capture card, it's worth exploring if you're serious about delivering top-tier performance.

Next, focus on your microphone. While built-in microphones might be sufficient for casual calls, streaming requires better audio clarity to keep viewers engaged. Affordable options like the Samson Meteor or the Blue Snowball are excellent for beginners, while professionals might opt for the Blue Yeti or Elgato Wave:3 for superior sound. A crisp, clear voice can often outweigh minor visual imperfections, making this a worthwhile investment early on.

Then, there's the webcam. Your camera brings your personality to life, helping viewers connect with you on a deeper level. If you're starting with a budget, a Logitech C920 or C922 webcam is a popular choice for its balance of affordability and quality. For those looking to elevate their visuals, DSLR cameras with capture cards provide professional-level video quality, though they require a larger upfront investment. Remember, your camera doesn't need to be the most expensive; it just needs to present you in a well-lit and inviting way.

Finally, your internet connection is the lifeblood of your stream. A strong, stable connection prevents buffering and keeps your stream looking sharp. Aim for an upload speed of at least 5 Mbps for 720p streaming and 10 Mbps for 1080p. Use a wired Ethernet connection wherever possible for maximum stability, and test your speed regularly to ensure you're meeting your platform's requirements.

Optimizing these components ensures your stream not only works but shines. For example, investing in a quality microphone and stable internet connection will often matter more to viewers than high-end visuals, especially when starting. The goal is to create a smooth, enjoyable experience that encourages your audience to stick around.

Your streaming setup is the bridge between your creative ideas and the audience eager to experience them. Whether you're starting with a simple laptop and a budget microphone or investing in a professional-grade rig, remember that it's not about having the flashiest equipment—it's about delivering value and connecting with your viewers.

For beginners, starting small and focusing on the essentials—like clear audio and stable internet—is often the smartest move. You can always upgrade as you grow, adding higher-quality peripherals or enhancing your visuals to match your evolving goals. For those aiming to hit the ground running with a professional setup, investing wisely in key areas like your microphone, camera, and internet reliability will pay dividends in creating a polished and engaging stream.

With your hardware ready, it's time to focus on the software that brings your stream to life. In the next chapter, we'll explore the tools of the trade, from OBS Studio to multistreaming platforms, and how to make the most of them to produce smooth, high-quality content. The pieces are coming together—let's get ready to go live!

Chapter 5: Choosing and Using Streaming Software

Behind every great live stream is a powerful piece of software working quietly in the background to bring it all together. Known as encoders, streaming software takes the raw video and audio from your computer or camera and converts it into a format that can be broadcast to platforms like Twitch, YouTube, or TikTok. Without this essential tool, your stream simply wouldn't exist.

For most streamers, **OBS Studio** (Open Broadcaster Software) is the gold standard. It's free, open-source, and packed with features to help you customize and control your streams. OBS gives you the ability to manage multiple video and audio sources, add overlays and transitions, and stream to just about any platform. It's highly versatile, making it a favorite among beginners and professionals alike.

If you're looking for simplicity without sacrificing functionality, **Restream Studio** is another excellent option. Unlike OBS, Restream runs directly in your browser, eliminating the need for downloads or complex installations. It's perfect for streamers who want to multistream to several platforms at once, manage viewer chats in real time, or easily invite guests to join their stream.

Choosing the right software is a critical step in building your streaming setup, and it all comes down to your goals and level of experience. Are you aiming for a polished, professional look? Do you want to stream to multiple platforms at once? Or do you just need a straightforward way to get started? The right software will be your partner in delivering high-quality content that resonates with your audience.

Once you've chosen your streaming software, the next step is learning how to use it effectively. Let's start with **OBS Studio**, one of the most widely used tools in the streaming world. Setting up OBS might seem intimidating at first, but breaking it into manageable steps makes the process straightforward.

- **Download and Install OBS**: Head to the OBS Studio website, download the software, and install it on your computer. Once installed, you'll be greeted by the main dashboard, which is your command center for managing all aspects of your stream.

- **Configure Settings**: Start by adjusting the settings to optimize performance. Navigate to the settings menu and choose a resolution (usually 720p or 1080p) and a frame rate (30fps or 60fps) that matches your PC's capabilities and internet speed. Set the bitrate to ensure smooth streaming—around 2,500 to 5,000 Kbps is standard for 1080p. OBS also allows you to choose between software and hardware encoding. If you have a dedicated GPU, select hardware encoding for better performance.

- **Set Up Scenes and Sources**: In OBS, a "scene" is like a canvas where you arrange your video, audio, and graphics. Add "sources" to your scenes, such as your webcam, microphone, or gameplay feed. You can also include custom overlays, logos, or widgets to give your stream a professional touch. For example, you might have one scene for your starting screen, another for live gameplay, and a third for an intermission screen.

- **Test Your Stream**: Before going live, always run a private test stream. This allows you to check audio levels, video clarity, and overall performance. OBS has a built-in recording feature that lets you capture and review test footage to identify and fix any issues before your audience sees them.

For streamers who want to take things to the next level, Restream Studio offers unique benefits. It's an ideal choice if you're planning to stream to multiple platforms simultaneously. Restream simplifies multistreaming, allowing you to broadcast to Twitch, YouTube, Facebook, and more—all at once. It also provides integrated tools for managing chats across platforms, so you can keep up with viewers no matter where they're watching.

Beyond these two options, there are other tools to explore based on your needs. Streamlabs OBS is a user-friendly version of OBS with added features like built-in themes and integrated alerts. If you're looking for browser-based simplicity, Restream Studio's interface makes it accessible for streamers who don't want to deal with complex installations. Each option has its strengths, and it's worth experimenting to see what fits your workflow best.

The features of streaming software go far beyond simply capturing video and audio. From adding overlays and transitions to managing multiple chat streams in real time, these tools allow you to create polished, engaging content. The more you explore the features, the more you'll discover how to elevate your streams and create a unique experience for your audience.

Mastering your streaming software is a process that evolves over time. The key is to start simple—focus on the basics like setting up your scenes, managing your audio levels, and getting comfortable with the interface. As you gain confidence, you can begin exploring advanced features like overlays, multistreaming, and interactive widgets to add personality and polish to your broadcasts.

Remember, practice is your best teacher. Spend time experimenting with your software before you go live, and don't hesitate to watch tutorials or seek advice from other streamers. OBS Studio, Restream Studio, and similar tools are incredibly powerful, but they're also intuitive once you've put in the time to learn how they work. The more familiar you are with your software, the smoother and more professional your streams will feel—not just to you but to your audience.

With your software toolkit in place, you're ready to connect it to your streaming platform of choice. In the next chapter, we'll explore the many options available—Twitch, YouTube Live, TikTok, and more—and how to choose the one (or ones) that align best with your goals and audience. Your streaming journey is about to reach new heights!

Chapter 6: Selecting Your Streaming Platform

Choosing the right platform is one of the most important decisions you'll make as a streamer. Each platform comes with its unique strengths, audiences, and features, which means finding the one that aligns with your content and goals can make all the difference. The streaming landscape today is vibrant and competitive, with platforms catering to almost every type of creator, whether you're a gamer, artist, educator, or business professional.

For many streamers, Twitch is the obvious choice, especially for gaming and creative content. Known for its interactive community features, Twitch allows streamers to connect directly with their audience through chat, emotes, and channel points, fostering a loyal viewer base. However, Twitch's popularity is both a blessing and a challenge. With thousands of creators streaming simultaneously, standing out can be difficult for new streamers. Success on Twitch often hinges on finding a niche and actively participating in the platform's community.

YouTube Live offers a more versatile option, especially for creators who blend live streams with pre-recorded videos. Its integration with the broader YouTube ecosystem means that streams don't just disappear after the session ends—they remain discoverable through YouTube's powerful search algorithms. This makes YouTube Live particularly attractive for tutorial-based content, educational streams, and long-form discussions. For instance, an artist might use YouTube Live to host interactive painting sessions and then edit those streams into time-lapse videos for on-demand viewers.

Meanwhile, TikTok Live has surged in popularity among mobile-first creators and younger audiences. Its algorithm-driven discoverability can introduce your content to new viewers faster than almost any other platform. Streamers who focus on interactive or short-form content, such as IRL (in real life) streams, Q&A sessions, or quick tutorials, have found significant success on TikTok Live. However, because of its fast-paced environment, building long-term relationships with viewers often requires pairing TikTok with a more community-focused platform like Twitch or YouTube.

For professionals, LinkedIn Live is a niche but powerful tool. This platform is perfect for hosting webinars, sharing career insights, or presenting live product demonstrations. It caters to professionals and thought leaders, making it an excellent choice if your goal is to network within your industry or establish yourself as an expert in your field. While its audience may be smaller compared to Twitch or YouTube, the level of engagement and credibility it provides can be unmatched for certain niches.

Facebook Live rounds out the major players as a platform with incredible reach. With billions of users worldwide, it's a strong option for creators targeting broad or community-driven content. Whether it's streaming local events, family-friendly activities, or fitness classes, Facebook Live's integration with groups and pages makes it easy to build a following among highly specific audiences. However, like other platforms, competition can be steep, and success often requires a solid promotion strategy.

No discussion of streaming platforms would be complete without mentioning the growing trend of multistreaming. Tools like Restream allow you to broadcast to multiple platforms simultaneously, such as Twitch, YouTube, and Facebook Live. Multistreaming is particularly useful for new creators who want to experiment with different platforms to see where their content resonates most. While it can dilute engagement on any single platform, it's an excellent way to maximize reach and diversify your audience from the start.

Let's take a look at how successful streamers use platforms strategically. For example, one gamer might start by streaming gameplay exclusively on Twitch to build a strong core audience. Later, they could expand to YouTube Live, using the platform for tutorials and game reviews to attract a wider audience. On the other hand, a fitness trainer might begin with short, high-energy TikTok Live sessions to attract new viewers, then direct them to Facebook Live for longer, more in-depth workouts. These approaches show how understanding the strengths of each platform can create a cohesive strategy for growth.

When deciding which platform is right for you, ask yourself: Where does my audience spend their time? What kind of experience am I trying to create? A gamer who thrives on interactive chat will feel at home on Twitch, while an educator might find YouTube Live's searchability indispensable for reaching learners. For creators targeting multiple demographics, multistreaming can offer the best of all worlds.

Selecting a platform—or a combination of platforms—isn't just a technical decision; it's a strategic one that shapes how you connect with your audience. By aligning your content with the right platform, you're setting the stage for meaningful engagement and sustained growth. But don't feel pressured to have everything perfect from the start. Many creators begin on one platform and expand over time, adapting as their content evolves and their audience grows.

Starting small is often the smartest move. Focusing on one platform lets you learn the nuances of streaming without spreading yourself too thin. Once you're comfortable, tools like Restream can help you scale your reach by broadcasting across multiple platforms simultaneously. This flexibility allows you to experiment and adjust your strategy without losing momentum.

With your platform chosen, the next step is ensuring that your setup and content are ready to shine. In the following chapter, we'll cover the critical final steps: testing your stream, troubleshooting potential issues, and building the confidence to hit that "Go Live" button. Your audience is waiting—let's make sure your debut is a smooth one.

Chapter 7: Testing and Going Live

Going live for the first time can be both exhilarating and nerve-wracking. However, even the most seasoned streamers will tell you that preparation is key to a successful broadcast. Testing your equipment and setup beforehand isn't just a good idea—it's essential. Skipping this step can lead to technical hiccups that might frustrate you and your audience, and it could derail an otherwise great stream.

Beginner streamers often underestimate how much can go wrong during a live broadcast. Common mistakes include mismatched audio and video, poor lighting, dropped frames due to weak internet connections, and even forgetting to hit the "Go Live" button properly. These errors are completely normal for first-timers, but most of them are avoidable with thorough testing.

By taking the time to test your setup, you not only catch potential problems but also build your confidence. A simple trial run can help you feel more prepared, allowing you to focus on delivering great content instead of troubleshooting under pressure. Testing isn't about perfection—it's about setting yourself up for a smooth, enjoyable experience for both you and your viewers.

Testing your setup may sound straightforward, but there are several components to evaluate before hitting that "Go Live" button. Breaking it down into a checklist can make the process efficient and thorough. Let's go through the key elements you need to test:

- **Audio Quality**

1. Start with your microphone. Audio issues are one of the most common reasons viewers leave a stream, so make sure your voice is clear, balanced, and free from background noise. Use your streaming software to check audio levels and avoid distortion by keeping your microphone gain at an appropriate level. Test your sound by recording a short clip and playing it back to ensure everything sounds professional. If you're using background music, check that it complements your voice without overpowering it.

- **Video Clarity**

Your video feed is another critical component. Whether you're using a webcam or a DSLR camera, make sure it's positioned correctly and delivers a clear, sharp image. Lighting plays a big role here, so test your setup under the conditions you'll be streaming in. Avoid harsh shadows or dim environments by using natural light or investing in affordable ring lights or softboxes. Adjust your streaming software's resolution settings to balance quality and performance based on your internet connection and hardware capabilities.

- **Internet Stability**

A strong and stable internet connection is the lifeline of any live stream. Use tools like Speedtest to check your upload speed, which is more critical for streaming than download speed. Ideally, you'll want at least 5 Mbps for 720p streaming and 10 Mbps for 1080p. If possible, use a wired Ethernet connection rather than Wi-Fi to minimize the risk of dropped frames or interruptions. Streaming software often includes an indicator for dropped frames— watch for this during your test run.

- **Lighting and Environment**

Your stream's visual appeal extends beyond your camera. Evaluate your background to ensure it's clean, relevant, and free of distractions. If you're using a green screen, test your chroma key settings to ensure a smooth, professional look. Lighting is another often-overlooked factor. Position lights to evenly illuminate your face without creating glare or unflattering shadows. A well-lit stream not only looks better but also keeps your audience focused on you.

- **Overlay and Visual Elements**

If you're using overlays, alerts, or graphics, test them in your streaming software. Ensure your layout is clean and that alerts, such as notifications for new followers or tips, function properly. Overlays should enhance your stream without overwhelming the viewer. Run a quick mock stream to see how these elements appear in real-time and adjust as needed.

- **Private Test Stream**

Once you've checked the individual components, do a private test stream. Most platforms, like Twitch and YouTube Live, offer a way to go live privately or unlisted. This allows you to simulate the live experience without an actual audience. Use this opportunity to monitor how your stream looks and sounds in real-time. Watch for sync issues between audio and video, glitches, or lag.

- **Feedback from Friends or Early Viewers**

If you feel ready for an audience, invite a few trusted friends or early supporters to watch your test stream. They can provide valuable feedback on everything from audio clarity to camera angles. Having a fresh set of eyes helps catch details you might overlook and offers insight into how your stream feels from a viewer's perspective.

Testing is more than a one-time task—it's a habit. Even experienced streamers test their setups before every session to ensure everything runs smoothly. By making testing part of your routine, you'll avoid surprises and be better prepared to handle any challenges that arise during a live broadcast.

Testing your setup isn't just about catching errors—it's about building confidence. By taking the time to troubleshoot potential issues, you can focus on what really matters during your stream: connecting with your audience. Every test run brings you closer to understanding your equipment, refining your workflow, and delivering a professional-quality experience that keeps viewers coming back.

Remember, no stream will ever be perfect, and that's okay. Live streaming thrives on authenticity, and small imperfections can even make you more relatable to your audience. The key is to embrace the learning process, make adjustments as needed, and approach each stream with a mindset of continuous improvement.

As you prepare to go live, take pride in how far you've come. You've laid the groundwork, fine-tuned your setup, and practiced to ensure a smooth debut. Now it's time to hit that "Go Live" button and share your unique voice with the world. In the next chapter, we'll explore strategies for engaging with your audience, creating a sense of community, and keeping viewers excited for your future streams. The journey is just beginning!

Chapter 8: Engaging with Your Audience

In the world of streaming, the audience is your greatest asset. Whether you're talking to one viewer or a thousand, every interaction matters. Engaging with your audience isn't just about filling the silence; it's about creating a connection that keeps people coming back. Viewers who feel seen, heard, and appreciated are more likely to stick around, support your stream, and tell others about you.

Think about what draws people to live streams in the first place. Unlike pre-recorded videos, streaming offers real-time interaction. It's an opportunity for viewers to participate directly in the experience, ask questions, and even shape the content as it unfolds. This dynamic creates a sense of belonging that no other medium can replicate. Your audience isn't just watching; they're part of the show.

Look at some of the most successful streamers today—what do they all have in common? It's not just their gaming skills or production value; it's the way they engage with their community. Streamers like Pokimane, who consistently interacts with her chat, or Ludwig, who involves viewers in his content decisions, showcase the power of building a loyal audience. Their streams feel like a conversation, not a one-sided broadcast, which is why their communities thrive.

Engagement goes beyond simply acknowledging your viewers. It's about creating a welcoming environment where people feel like part of something bigger. Whether it's greeting viewers by name, answering questions, or reacting to comments in real time, small gestures can make a big impact. The key is to be present, authentic, and approachable, no matter the size of your audience.

A well-engaged audience can also elevate your content. They'll give you real-time feedback, share ideas, and even provide the energy that makes streaming so rewarding. But to harness this power, you must genuinely invest in your community. Think of your stream as a gathering space, not just a performance. The more you include your viewers, the more connected they'll feel—and the more likely they are to return.

Engaging with your audience isn't just a best practice; it's a necessity for growth. Streamers who ignore their chat or treat viewers as passive observers often struggle to build a loyal following. On the flip side, even a small streamer who takes the time to interact can create a tight-knit community that grows organically. Viewers who feel appreciated are your best advocates, spreading the word about your stream to friends and online communities.

To cultivate meaningful engagement, it's important to approach your audience with genuine curiosity and gratitude. Ask questions, spark discussions, and let your personality shine. Remember, people come to streams not just for the content, but for the streamer. Your unique energy and perspective are what will set you apart and keep viewers invested.

Once you understand the value of audience interaction, the next step is learning how to engage effectively. Successful engagement isn't about simply acknowledging your viewers—it's about building relationships that make them feel like an essential part of your stream. Here's how to do that.

1. Engaging in Chat

The chat box is the heartbeat of your stream. Whether it's buzzing with activity or sparsely populated, treat it as your direct line to your viewers. Respond to comments, answer questions, and acknowledge new followers or subscribers. Even a simple "Hey, welcome to the stream!" can make someone's day.

To keep the energy high, encourage participation by asking open-ended questions like, "What's everyone playing this week?" or "What's your favorite character in this game?" These questions not only spark conversation but also show your audience that you value their input. As you grow, it might become difficult to respond to every message, but prioritizing engagement—even in small ways—goes a long way toward building loyalty.

2. Building Rapport

Interaction is more than just words; it's about the tone and authenticity you bring to your stream. Share stories, let your personality shine, and be willing to laugh at yourself. The best streamers create a sense of camaraderie by being relatable and approachable. If viewers see you as someone they'd enjoy hanging out with, they're more likely to stick around and even bring their friends.

Another effective way to build rapport is to remember recurring viewers. If someone consistently shows up in chat, make a point to recognize them. Saying something like, "Hey, Sarah! Glad you're here again!" creates a sense of belonging that turns casual viewers into regulars.

3. Handling Negative Comments or Trolls

Not every interaction will be positive, and it's crucial to handle negativity professionally. Trolls and inappropriate comments are an unfortunate reality of streaming, but how you respond can set the tone for your community.

The golden rule? Don't feed the trolls. Instead of engaging with negativity, calmly address inappropriate behavior or use moderation tools to remove offensive comments. Many platforms allow you to assign moderators or use bots to filter out problematic messages automatically. By maintaining a welcoming and respectful environment, you signal to your audience that your stream is a safe and enjoyable space for everyone.

4. Creating a Sense of Community

Engagement extends beyond individual interactions—it's about fostering a collective identity for your audience. Use inclusive language like "we" and "us" to make viewers feel like they're part of a group. You can also create inside jokes, use nicknames for your community, or come up with fun traditions that make your stream feel unique.

Another powerful way to build community is through consistent interaction. Consider hosting special events like Q&A sessions, gaming challenges, or giveaways. These activities encourage viewers to participate actively and create shared experiences that strengthen their connection to your stream.

5. Leveraging Social Media for Engagement

Your audience engagement doesn't have to stop when the stream ends. Use social media to keep the conversation going, whether by responding to comments, sharing highlights from your streams, or posting polls to involve your audience in future content decisions. Platforms like Twitter, Instagram, and Discord can become extensions of your community, helping you maintain momentum between streams.

6. Inviting Collaboration

Collaboration is another great way to engage your audience. Invite viewers to join your games, participate in polls, or submit ideas for your stream. For instance, you might let viewers choose the next game you'll play or vote on in-stream challenges. These opportunities for direct involvement create a sense of ownership among your audience, making them more invested in your success.

7. Learning from Viewer Feedback

Your audience is one of your greatest resources for improvement. Encourage viewers to share feedback on what they love about your stream and what could be better. You can even set up anonymous polls or surveys for honest input. By acting on their suggestions, you show your audience that their opinions matter, which deepens their loyalty to your channel.

8. Balancing Interaction and Content

While engagement is crucial, it's also important to balance interaction with delivering high-quality content. Over-responding to chat can sometimes disrupt the flow of your stream, especially during gameplay or structured discussions. The trick is to find a rhythm that allows you to stay connected with your audience while maintaining focus on your primary content.

Professional streamers often designate specific moments to engage, such as during breaks or loading screens. Others use features like chat highlights to prioritize key messages without overwhelming the stream. Experiment with different approaches to find what works best for your style.

Engaging with your audience is both an art and a science. By mastering the fundamentals—chat interaction, community-building, and professional conflict management—you can turn casual viewers into loyal supporters. The more effort you invest in fostering these relationships, the more rewarding your streaming journey will be.

Chapter 9: Growing Your Audience

Building an audience in the ever-expanding world of live streaming can feel like trying to stand out in a crowded stadium. With millions of creators vying for attention, it's no wonder new streamers often feel overwhelmed by the competition. But the good news is that a loyal audience isn't built overnight—it's built through consistent effort, authentic connection, and smart promotion.

At its core, audience growth requires you to balance two key elements: creating great content and ensuring people know about it. This is where the concept of self-promotion comes in. For many creators, the idea of promoting themselves can feel uncomfortable or even cringeworthy. However, the truth is that even the best streams can go unnoticed without effective outreach. Self-promotion isn't about bragging; it's about sharing your passion and inviting others to be part of it.

In a landscape where algorithms often decide who gets noticed, learning how to make your content discoverable is essential. Whether through social media, networking, or optimizing your stream titles, the effort you put into reaching potential viewers is just as important as the effort you put into your actual stream. It's not about shouting into the void; it's about finding the people who will resonate with your work and building genuine relationships with them.

Once you've embraced the concept of self-promotion, it's time to implement strategies to expand your reach. Growing your audience isn't just about working harder—it's about working smarter. Here are some proven approaches to make your content more discoverable and appealing to potential viewers.

Social media platforms are some of the most powerful tools for streamers. Platforms like X (formerly Twitter), Instagram, TikTok, and even LinkedIn can serve as gateways to your content. To promote your streams effectively, focus on creating engaging posts that capture attention quickly. Use eye-catching visuals, short video snippets, or teaser images that give potential viewers a reason to click through to your stream.

A great strategy is repurposing your live content into highlights. Did you have a hilarious moment or a jaw-dropping play during your stream? Clip it, edit it, and post it as a standalone piece of content. These bite-sized previews allow people unfamiliar with your channel to sample your style and personality. Platforms like TikTok and Instagram Reels are particularly effective for short, engaging clips that can go viral and drive traffic back to your stream.

Consistency is also key. Posting regularly keeps your audience engaged and increases the likelihood of new viewers discovering your content. Create a schedule for your social media posts, just like you would for your streams, and stick to it. Regular updates, countdowns to your next stream, and follow-up posts can keep your content fresh and visible.

Search Engine Optimization (SEO) isn't just for websites—it's also a crucial part of growing your streaming audience. Platforms like YouTube and Twitch rely on keywords to categorize and recommend content. By using trendy titles and descriptive tags, you can increase your stream's visibility.

For example, instead of titling your stream "Chill Gaming Night," try something more specific and searchable, like "Top 10 Survival Strategies in Minecraft – Live Gameplay." Pair your title with a strong description and relevant tags that include keywords your audience might search for. On platforms like YouTube, adding timestamps to your videos can also improve engagement and retention.

Don't forget about hashtags. Platforms like TikTok, Instagram, and Twitter thrive on hashtag use. Research trending hashtags relevant to your content and incorporate them into your posts. Tools like Hashtagify can help you identify high-performing hashtags that align with your niche.

One of the fastest ways to expand your audience is by teaming up with other streamers. Collaboration introduces you to a new set of viewers who are already engaged with similar content. Look for creators who share your niche but aren't direct competitors, and propose collaborative events like co-streams, interviews, or gaming sessions.

When collaborating, focus on creating content that benefits both parties. For example, if you're a gamer, team up with another streamer to play a multiplayer game. If you're an artist, consider a dual art challenge where each of you works on a different interpretation of the same theme. These collaborations are not only fun but also help you cross-pollinate audiences.

Networking at industry events, virtual meetups, or even within online communities can also lead to collaboration opportunities. The key is to approach potential collaborators with genuine interest and a clear value proposition. Let them know what you bring to the table and how working together can be mutually beneficial.

Your audience doesn't stop being your audience when your stream ends. Use tools like Discord servers, private Facebook groups, or email newsletters to keep the conversation going between streams. These platforms allow you to foster deeper relationships with your community and keep them invested in your journey.

For instance, a Discord server can serve as a hub for your viewers to interact, share memes, and discuss topics related to your content. By participating in these conversations, you show your audience that you value their input and appreciate their presence. Exclusive updates, sneak peeks, or behind-the-scenes content can make your audience feel like insiders.

Hosting events like giveaways, tournaments, or themed streams can be a great way to attract new viewers. For example, offering a small prize for a giveaway—such as a game code, merch, or a shoutout—can incentivize people to share your stream with their friends. Similarly, hosting a special event like a charity stream or milestone celebration can generate buzz and bring in a wider audience.

While these events require some planning, the payoff in terms of engagement and reach is often well worth the effort. Just make sure to follow platform guidelines when running giveaways or contests to avoid any issues.

Don't limit yourself to a single streaming platform. Tools like Restream allow you to broadcast to multiple platforms simultaneously, giving you access to diverse audiences. This strategy is particularly effective if you're still trying to figure out where your content resonates most.

For instance, you might find that your gaming streams perform best on Twitch, while your tutorials gain traction on YouTube. Experimenting with different platforms lets you tailor your content strategy to maximize reach and engagement.

Understanding your audience means knowing what works and what doesn't. Platforms like Twitch, YouTube, and Facebook provide analytics tools that let you track key metrics, such as average viewership, chat activity, and retention rates. Use this data to identify trends and adjust your strategy accordingly.

For example, if you notice a spike in viewers during a specific type of content, consider incorporating more of that into your streams. If retention rates drop at certain points, analyze what might be causing viewers to lose interest and make improvements.

While these strategies are essential, remember that authenticity remains the cornerstone of audience growth. People are drawn to streamers who are genuine and relatable. Don't try to mimic someone else's style or force a persona that doesn't feel true to who you are. Instead, focus on showcasing your unique perspective and personality.

Your audience will grow not just because of your promotional efforts but because they feel a connection to you. As long as you stay true to yourself, the viewers who resonate with your content will find you—and they'll stick around.

Growing an audience takes time, persistence, and a willingness to adapt. It's not just about following a checklist—it's about creating a presence that people genuinely want to be part of. By leveraging social media, optimizing your content for discoverability, collaborating with others, and engaging with your community both on and off your stream, you can steadily expand your reach and cultivate a loyal following.

Remember, there's no single "right" way to grow your audience. What works for one streamer might not work for another. The key is to experiment with different strategies, analyze what resonates with your viewers, and refine your approach over time. Growth isn't linear, and setbacks are part of the process, but each step you take brings you closer to building the thriving community you envision.

As you implement these strategies, always keep your authenticity front and center. Viewers are drawn to streamers who are passionate, relatable, and real. It's your unique personality that will set you apart in a crowded landscape. Growth is important, but never let it come at the cost of losing sight of who you are or why you started streaming in the first place.

With a growing audience comes new opportunities and challenges. In the next chapter, we'll explore how to sustain your success by maintaining consistency and analyzing your performance. From learning how to interpret analytics to avoiding burnout, you'll gain the tools you need to keep your momentum going and turn your streaming journey into a long-term success story. The best is yet to come!

Chapter 10: Sustaining Success and Analyzing Performance

Reaching an audience is an accomplishment, but keeping them engaged over the long term is what truly defines a successful streamer. Sustaining your success requires more than just showing up—it demands consistency, a keen eye for improvement, and the ability to adapt to changing circumstances. The most successful streamers are those who treat streaming as both an art and a science, blending creativity with data-driven decision-making.

One of the most critical aspects of long-term success is consistency. Viewers thrive on predictability, and a regular streaming schedule builds trust and anticipation within your audience. When people know when and where to find you, they're more likely to incorporate your streams into their routines. But consistency isn't just about time; it's about quality. Delivering high-value content every time you go live reinforces your reputation as a reliable and engaging creator.

Equally important is your ability to analyze and refine your approach. Metrics like viewership, average watch time, and chat engagement offer valuable insights into what's working and what's not. These numbers tell a story about your audience—when they're most active, what type of content they enjoy, and where you might be losing their attention. Learning to interpret these metrics allows you to make informed decisions that keep your streams relevant and captivating.

Streaming is a journey of continuous learning, and every broadcast is an opportunity to grow. By committing to both consistency and thoughtful analysis, you can turn a fledgling audience into a thriving community and ensure your streaming career stands the test of time.

Sustaining success as a streamer requires more than just creativity and consistency—it demands the ability to measure your progress and adapt based on what you learn. This is where analytics becomes invaluable. Numbers might not seem exciting, but they hold the key to unlocking your potential and keeping your streams relevant in an ever-changing landscape.

Most major streaming platforms, like Twitch, YouTube, and Facebook, provide built-in analytics tools. These tools can give you detailed insights into your performance, showing you metrics like average viewership, peak viewership, engagement rate, and watch time. Understanding these numbers helps you answer crucial questions: When is your audience most active? Which content resonates the most? At what point do viewers tend to drop off?

Start by focusing on key metrics. Average viewership tells you how many people are tuning in, while engagement metrics (like chat activity) show how invested those viewers are in your content. Retention rate is another critical metric—it measures how long viewers stick around, which can signal whether your stream pacing and content are holding their attention.

For example, if you notice a consistent dip in viewers after the first 20 minutes of your streams, it might indicate a need to tighten your introduction or get to the core of your content faster. Conversely, a spike in chat activity during a specific segment can highlight the parts of your stream that your audience finds most engaging, giving you a template for future content.

Platforms like Twitch provide heat maps of viewer activity, showing the times when your audience is most engaged. Use this data to fine-tune your streaming schedule. If your peak viewership consistently occurs during evening hours, consider shifting your streams to maximize that window.

Analytics are only useful if you act on them. Once you've identified trends in your data, use those insights to adapt your content. Let's say your metrics show that streams featuring a particular game or activity consistently outperform others. This is a clear sign to lean into that niche while still experimenting to keep things fresh.

Adaptation doesn't mean abandoning your interests. Instead, find ways to balance audience preferences with your creative vision. If your viewers love interactive segments, you might add more polls or Q&A sessions to your streams. If they're drawn to your gameplay of a certain title, consider building a series around it. By aligning your content with audience preferences, you create a cycle of engagement that benefits both you and your community.

Data can also help you refine your stream's format. If viewers drop off after an hour, it might be worth experimenting with shorter streams. On the other hand, if longer streams show better retention, consider extending your sessions. The key is to remain flexible and willing to try new approaches based on what the data tells you.

As rewarding as streaming can be, it's also demanding. The pressure to perform, coupled with the unpredictable nature of audience growth, can lead to burnout if you're not careful. Burnout not only affects your mental and physical health but can also disrupt your content quality and consistency.

One of the most effective ways to prevent burnout is to establish boundaries. Streaming should be a part of your life, not your entire life. Set a schedule that allows for downtime, and resist the urge to stream every waking moment. Consistency is important, but so is sustainability.

Another critical factor is managing your workload. While it's tempting to handle every aspect of your stream solo, outsourcing tasks like video editing, graphic design, or even moderation can free up your time and reduce stress. Many streamers also use tools like scheduling software or chatbots to automate repetitive tasks, leaving more room for creativity and engagement.

Make time for self-care. Regular exercise, a balanced diet, and quality sleep aren't just good for your health—they directly impact your energy levels and on-camera presence. Remember, your audience is tuning in for *you*, and taking care of yourself ensures that you can bring your best to every stream.

While analytics and adaptation are crucial, they won't mean much if you're stretched too thin. Time management is a skill every successful streamer must master. This involves not only planning your streams but also allocating time for preparation, promotion, and post-stream follow-up.

Use tools like calendars or task management apps to organize your schedule. Block out time for scripting or outlining your content, setting up your equipment, and interacting with your community between streams. Treat streaming like any other professional commitment, with clearly defined work hours and goals.

Effective time management also includes knowing when to take a step back. It's easy to fall into the trap of overcommitting, especially when you're passionate about your craft. Remember, long-term success depends on maintaining a steady pace, not sprinting to exhaustion.

One of the most effective ways to sustain success is to establish a feedback loop with your audience. Encourage viewers to share their thoughts about your streams—what they love, what they'd like to see more of, and what could be improved. Use tools like surveys, polls, or even direct chat interactions to gather this feedback.

Audience feedback often complements the data you gather from analytics, providing qualitative insights that numbers alone can't reveal. For instance, viewers might point out that they enjoy your sense of humor or your storytelling, even if those elements don't show up in metrics like watch time. By combining data with feedback, you can make more nuanced decisions about your content strategy.

Ultimately, sustaining success is about finding a balance—between data and creativity, engagement and self-care, experimentation and consistency. By leveraging analytics, adapting your content, and protecting your mental health, you can keep your streams relevant and enjoyable for both you and your audience.

Success in streaming isn't a destination—it's a journey that evolves with time, effort, and a willingness to grow. Continuous learning and adaptability are your greatest allies in this ever-changing landscape. The streaming world is dynamic, with new tools, trends, and challenges emerging constantly. The most successful creators are those who embrace this change, remaining open to feedback, experimentation, and self-improvement.

Remember, streaming is as much about the journey as it is about the results. Celebrate your wins, no matter how small, and learn from your setbacks without letting them define you. Every stream is an opportunity to connect, create, and refine your craft. Whether you're analyzing your metrics, brainstorming fresh content ideas, or taking a well-deserved break, each step you take is an investment in your long-term success.

Above all, stay true to why you started streaming in the first place. Authenticity, passion, and perseverance are what draw people to you—and what keep them coming back. Your unique voice and perspective are your greatest assets. Share them boldly, and trust that the right audience will find you.

The road to sustained success may be challenging, but it's also incredibly rewarding. So, keep learning, keep adapting, and, most importantly, keep enjoying the process. Your journey as a streamer is uniquely yours—embrace it, and let your growth inspire others.

A Word from the Author

First and foremost, thank you for picking up this book. Whether you're a complete beginner or someone looking to take your streaming journey to the next level, I'm honored that you've chosen to spend your time with my words. Streaming is a unique and exciting adventure, and I'm thrilled to play even a small part in your journey.

This book is the result of countless hours of research, observation, and trial and error—not just my own, but from learning alongside creators who've shared their triumphs and struggles. My hope is that the strategies, tips, and insights within these pages empower you to navigate the streaming world with confidence and creativity.

Remember, every successful streamer started somewhere. Every viral moment, thriving community, or exciting milestone began with a single stream and a simple idea: to share something meaningful with the world. No matter where you are on your journey, you have something valuable to offer. Your unique voice, perspective, and passion are what will make your streams stand out.

Streaming is as much about the experience as it is about the outcomes. It's about connecting with people, sharing your story, and enjoying the process of growth. There will be challenges, but there will also be moments of incredible joy and fulfillment. Stay dedicated, embrace the lessons, and never stop learning.

I wish you the best of luck as you hit that "Go Live" button and start building something truly special. Whether your goal is to share your passion, create a thriving community, or even make streaming a career, you've got what it takes to succeed.

Here's to your streaming journey—may it be full of discovery, creativity, and connection.

Jordan Vance

www.ingramcontent.com/pod-product-compliance
Lightning Source LLC
LaVergne TN
LVHW060125070326

832902LV00019B/3140